Take A Tree Walk

By Jane Kirkland
with
Rob Kirkland
Dorothy Burke
Melanie Palaisa

Ready?

You're about to set out on a tree walk adventure! You'll make new discoveries and see things you haven't noticed before. Then you can help to complete this unfinished book, and only **you** can finish it.

What's a tree walk adventure? Well, I had one while riding my bike through a neighborhood near my house. I saw this very large oak tree. It was the biggest oak tree I'd ever seen! I was so amazed by this tree that I now visit often to take pictures in winter, summer, spring, and fall.

Last winter I met the family who owns the property. They call their tree "Corny Whitey" because it's a White Oak tree with acorns. Located in the middle of the neighborhood, Corny is home to birds, squirrels, raccoons and insects, as well as a popular place for neighbors to visit and swing on the swing that hangs from Corny's large branches. Have you ever seen such an amazing tree?

This large oak is a White Oak. It's over 235 years old! The oak tree is the state tree of Iowa. The White Oak is the state tree of Connecticut, Illinois, and Maryland and the Live Oak is the state tree of Georgia.

What Is a Tree Walk?

A tree walk is an adventure you take to find and identify trees. A great place to start is in your own backyard. You can walk alone or with your friends, brothers or sisters, parents, or even the whole family! You can also take a tree walk in your schoolyard with your classmates and teacher.

Where to Go—What to Wear

Your backyard might be a good place to take your first tree walk but if there are no trees nearby, take this walk in a local park, in a schoolyard, or in a friend's backyard. Take this book with you when you travel to see friends and relatives or when you are on vacation.

If it's very cold outside, bundle up in layers of warm clothes and wear shoes or boots that will keep your feet warm and dry. If it's raining, don't forget to wear your raincoat. If you see lightning, do NOT stand under a tree—go indoors immediately! If it's a sunny day, wear lotion that protects your skin from the sun. In warmer months be sure to wear something that protects you from insects.

Set?

Here's a list of items you might want to take with you on your walk along with this book and a pencil or pen. If you don't have everything on this list, don't worry. You can still have a great time. At some point, however, you will need a field guide to identify the trees you see.

✓ A bag to collect leaves, nuts, or seeds.

✓ A tree *field guide* (if you don't have one now, consider getting one later from a library or bookstore).

✓ If you want to measure the height or age of a tree today, bring a tape measure and a friend to help you. Don't worry, I'm not going to suggest you climb the tree to measure it ☺.

✓ A trash bag. You can put any trash you find in it and help keep the environment clean for all inhabitants—including you!

What will you do on your walk? Take this book along with you today and in the future each time you take a new tree walk. As you walk you can complete as much of this book as you want. You can also finish parts of this book at home after your walk. Here are some of the things you can do on your tree walk today:

✓ Take *field notes* and write down questions or thoughts you have about trees as you take your walk.

✓ Draw a map, draw pictures, or take photos of the trees you see.

✓ Identify the trees you find.

✓ Write a story about your exciting adventure.

What's a Field Guide?

A field guide is a book that helps identify things such as trees, birds, and mammals, just to name a few. A tree field guide helps you identify the trees you see by providing descriptions and photos of trees. There are many good tree field guides. Here are two of my favorites:

National Audubon Society Field Guide to North American Trees

Alfred A. Knopf, Publisher. Available for Eastern or Western regions.

An all-photograph field guide to trees. Find your tree by leaf shape, flowers, fruit, or fall leaves.

DK Pockets: Trees

By Theresa Greenaway. DK Pub Merchandise.

An easy-to-use and easy-to-carry field guide to trees.

What Are Field Notes?

Scientists, artists, and naturalists often take notes called "field notes" when doing research or while making observations. Their field notes are a record of such things as the date, the weather, and what they see. You can take field notes on your first tree walk. Then, when you take another tree walk at a different time of year, you can compare your old field notes with the new ones. You'll discover how trees change with the seasons.

Ready to meet some trees? Take this book and go outside to your backyard or to the place where you want to start your walk. Read as you go or read ahead of time, but don't forget to take the book.

This entire book is dedicated to helping you enjoy, appreciate and find out about trees. You'll see how to gather the information you need in order to identify (or "ID") trees. Trees are cool to observe at any time of the year. In winter, you see the bark and you can get a good idea of the shape. In spring you see budding leaves or flowers. In summer you see the leaves and fruit (if the tree has fruit), and in fall, depending on your location, you may see the wonderful fall colors of the leaves. Do you see leaves on the trees today? What season is it now?

Now stand very quietly for a moment and look around. Draw a map of your surroundings and mark the positions of the trees you see.

How Long Will This Take?

Your walk can be as short as 15 minutes or as long as several hours. People say "Time flies when you're having fun," and time will fly when you take a tree walk!

Questions?

If you have ideas or questions during your walk, write them down on page 30. After your walk, review your questions and ideas. Take your questions to your teacher or parents, or find the answers yourself at your library or by searching the Internet.

Here's An Idea

Do you know someone who might enjoy taking a tree walk with you but who can't come along? Perhaps your grandparents can't get around very well, or maybe you know someone who is ill or disabled. They can enjoy your walk if you share your book with them and your stories about the discoveries you made. Consider collecting leaves or pine cones for your friend.

Trees come in many shapes and sizes. Here are three very popular trees: (from left to right) the European Beech, Weeping Willow and American Basswood.

My Map

Here's an example of a map of a yard by someone who can't draw (me ☺). If you know the species of the trees you see, write that on your map. If you don't recognize the species, write an "X" or "?" next to that tree on your map. After you learn more about trees, you can come back to your map to label your tree species.

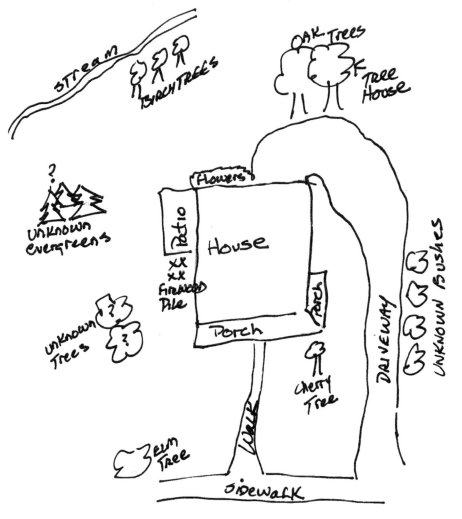

What to Draw:

If you're not artistic, draw boxes and circles to represent the things you see. Label your boxes with simple descriptions such as "house," "pine trees," and so forth.

Whether you're in a park, your backyard, or a schoolyard, here are items you may want to include on your map:

Trees or groups of trees and bushes.

Flower or food gardens.

Paths, sidewalks, buildings and parking lots.

Playground equipment.

Lakes, rivers, creeks, ponds, or swimming pools.

The yellows and oranges of fall are beautiful. From left to right the Black Maple, Yellow Poplar, Northern Red Oak, and Sugar Maple are wearing their fall colors. The Sugar Maple is the state tree for New York, West Virginia, Wisconsin, and Vermont.

Tree Families

Tree families are groups of related trees, like the maple family. Some tree families might surprise you; the oaks belong to the beech family! Many field guides are organized by tree families.

Will We Hear from You?

We enjoy hearing from our readers. Throughout this book you'll find stories written by our readers about their tree walks. We'd like to hear about your walk, too. Send your story to us and include artwork if you like. Let us know if you would like to see a Take a Walk Book about other topics. Our contact information is:

Take a Walk® Books

P. O. Box 500

Lionville, PA 19353

Email: Jane@takeawalk.com

Let's stop for a minute to think about the kinds of trees you know. Write down every kind of tree you can think of, like oak or maple. If you should see and recognize these trees today, return to this page and place a checkmark next to the tree name.

List the kinds of trees you know.

If you see a tree and don't know what species it is, you'll need to observe some things about that tree. As you read more of this book, you'll learn more about each of these items. But for now, take a moment to observe:

✓ The tree size and shape

✓ The leaf size, shape, and color

✓ The flowers (if there are any)

✓ The fruit (if there is any)

✓ The color and texture of the bark

✓ The location of the tree

Trees are great to climb on—in the summer with your friends—all the way to the fall.

By Kyle Jacobs and Matt Singer, both 8 years old.

Why Are Trees Important?

Can you imagine the world without trees? I can't! Trees are important to our environment for many reasons. Here are just a few:

- **Trees help us breathe.** As they remove carbon dioxide from the air, trees give back oxygen. Some trees can produce five pounds of oxygen per day!

- **Trees provide food.** Many of our fruits and nuts come from trees, such as apples, oranges, pecans, and pears. Can you name more? Many trees have berries and flowers that are an important food source for birds and other animals.

- **Trees provide shelter.** Trees are "home" to many creatures. Evergreens are particularly important to birds and other animals in cold winter months because they provide a protected area to rest or sleep.

- **Trees reduce soil erosion.** The roots of a tree help keep soil in place. When hard rains come, the roots help to keep the soil from washing away.

- **Trees provide materials.** We use materials made from trees to make paper, lumber, furniture, tools, and even boats. The Douglas Fir is one of the world's most important sources of lumber. It's also the state tree of Oregon.

- **Trees reduce energy needs.** Trees in your yard can provide shade in the summer to help keep your house cool. If they lose their leaves in winter, they let the sun shine through, which helps to keep your home warm. Evergreens can protect your house from wind and provide shelter for birds year round.

As you can see, trees are very useful. Can you think of any other reasons why trees are important?

Leave Only Footprints

When you take a walk, remember not to leave anything behind except your footprints. Don't drop trash where you go, and watch where you walk so you don't step on any flowers, garden plants, or small animals. Try not to disturb too many things around you. Stones and logs could be the homes of little creatures.

First Place Prize!

I think if there were a contest for the biggest bird nest found in trees, the bald eagles might win. Their nest of sticks can be as big as 10 feet across and 12 feet deep! That's because both mates return to their nest year after year, adding to it each year. If the nest gets so big it topples over or if a storm blows the nest down, they start building all over again in the same location.

New Word?

Species (SPEE-shees):

A certain kind, variety or type of living creature.

Find the State Trees

The state trees of all fifty states are named in this book. As you come across them, list them on page thirty. Hint: the first state tree appears on page two.

Don't Trees Start Out as Bushes?

No. Trees start out as saplings. Bushes are tree "wanna-bees". Although bushes are woody plants that can grow over 10 feet tall and have branches like trees, a bush doesn't have a trunk.

This elephant is a tree wanna-bee, too. He has a trunk and is dressed in leaves but he's not a real Elephant tree. An Elephant tree has a trunk that looks like the legs of a real elephant! The Elephant tree is a native of Arizona but it's not the state tree—the Paloverde is the Arizona state tree. Real elephants don't live in Arizona. They are natives of India and Africa.

What makes a tree a tree? Well, a tree is a perennial (per-EN-ee-ul) plant, which means it lives longer than two years. A tree has one main woody trunk from which many branches grow. Most trees grow taller than 10 feet. There are over 600 species of trees in North America. Some trees are deciduous (di-SID-jew-us) meaning that they lose their leaves in certain seasons. Other trees are evergreen; their leaves stay green all year.

Trees are divided into two groups: gymnosperms (JIM-no-sperms) and angiosperms (AN-jee-o-sperms). Gymnosperms include all the pine trees and trees similar to pines such as spruce and cypress. The seeds of the gymnosperm trees are contained in cones, such as pinecones. The more common name for gymnosperms is conifers (CON-if-ers), which means cone-bearing (having cones).

Angiosperms include all the trees that are not conifers (not cone-bearing) such as maples and oaks. Angiosperm trees are commonly called broadleaf trees because they have wide, flat leaves. The seeds of a broadleaf tree are contained in its fruit, which can be a berry, a fleshy fruit like a peach, an acorn, a nut, or even a pod.

Whether a tree is a conifer or broadleaf, seeds must be produced by the tree and planted (by animals, wind or people) so more trees will grow. Can you tell which of the trees you see were planted by man and which are growing naturally?

Each **species** of tree has its own needs and must have the right habitat. A habitat (HAB-i-tat) is the part of the environment in which one lives; like the desert or the forest. The species of trees you find today depends on the environment and habitat of your location. Write about your habitat in your field notes on the facing page.

My Field Notes

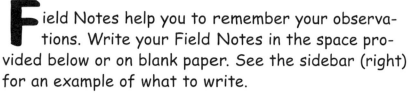

Field Notes help you to remember your observations. Write your Field Notes in the space provided below or on blank paper. See the sidebar (right) for an example of what to write.

What to Write

Your field notes should contain information specific to this day and this tree walk.

Be sure to include today's date and your location.

Write information about the weather; is the sun shining, is the sky cloudy, is it raining? If there's snow on the ground, write down how deep it is. Record the season and the current temperature if you know it.

If you recognize trees, write about them in your notes.

Write what you can now; you can write more after your walk.

September 29. 2PM. It is early autumn. Sunny with a few fluffy clouds. About 68 degrees. No wind. Chris and I are walking the bike trail on the west side of the lake at the park. We passed a meadow where we saw about 30 or 40 Monarch butterflies flitting around and a pair of Red-tailed Hawks in the sky. Some of the trees have started to turn and I can see red and yellow leaves in the woods. There are lots of different kinds of maples here. We'll collect maple leaves to study at home and look them up in our field guide. We saw some deer in the woods and we hear geese flying overhead.

A Family Affair

When Robbie Jennings (age 8), his sister Becca (age 11) and their Mom went on their first tree walk, here's what Robbie wrote:

"When we went on this walk we saw many different kinds of leaves and we had fun. It's interesting to learn about all the varieties of leaves and other things in nature. I like playing games outside because it gives me a new way to look at nature."

Hey, These Trees Have Cavities!

Chris Freas (age 9) invited his Mom to join him on his first tree walk and they walked for two hours! He wrote this observation about trees:

"When I was walking in the woods, I saw holes in trees. I thought they were caused by a woodpecker."

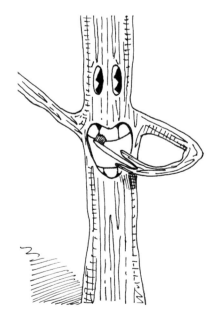

A tree can be a temporary or permanent home to many creatures. Some birds nest in trees; woodpeckers make a hole and build their nests in the hole. These holes are called cavities; the same word used to describe a hole in a tooth. Other birds build nests on top of branches, and some weave nests that hang below branches.

Mammals such as squirrels live in trees—but not all species of squirrels. Those that do live in trees make nests from leaves, or they live in natural holes, or old woodpecker holes. Raccoons live in trees, too. So do insects—can you think of any? How about termites?

Plants such as ferns, flowers, orchids, and mosses grow on trees. Different types of fungi, (FUN-ji) such as mushrooms and shelf fungi, also grow on trees.

Some owls nest in tree cavities but not the Great Horned Owl. This owl doesn't build a nest and doesn't nest in a cavity. Instead she takes over an old hawk, crow, or squirrel nest on the branches of a tree.

This is a type of shelf fungus. Shelf fungi usually grow on trees in moist, shady areas. If you walk in a shady forest, you might find some type of fungus growing on a tree.

...And On Trees?

Do you know of any amphibians that live in trees? Some species of treefrogs live in trees, but not all—go figure!

A woman named Julia Butterfly Hill once lived in a redwood tree in northern California. In 1997 Julia learned of plans

Found in the southern U.S. the Squirrel Treefrog is nicknamed the "rain frog" because he sometimes falls out of the sky while jumping through trees in search of insects.

to clear a three-acre parcel of ancient forest that included a 1000-year-old tree nicknamed "Luna." To save the tree and the forest, Julia and others began tree-sitting, actually living in the tree so no one could cut it down. Julia moved into the tree permanently. Her effort became inter-national news and, finally, after years of negotiation, the tree and its forest were saved. Thank you, Julia!

Can you think of any other creatures that live in trees?

At 180 feet, Luna is too tall to fit in this photo. Here's Julia at the top of Luna. She lived under the blue tarp for more than two years! The California Redwood is the state tree of California.

Making a Difference

Julia Butterfly Hill showed the world that one person could make a difference. Because of her efforts and the help of others, Luna and her forest are now protected for your generation and, hopefully, generations to come. What will you do to improve our world? Are you already making a difference?

Tree Names

Every tree has a scientific name and a common name. The Yellow Poplar is also called the "tuliptree" because its flowers are tulip shaped. Trees have only one scientific name but sometimes the same tree is known by different common names in different parts of the country. For example, the Southern Magnolia is also called the Bull-bay in one area of the country and the Evergreen Magnolia in another.

Dominic's Tree

Dominic Whitby (age 10) and his sister wrote this about their first tree walk:

"I like to see what evidence there is of wildlife living in and around the trees. I look for holes, squirrels, and chipmunks. I look at the bird nests to see if they are still inhabited or abandoned."

How Old Is That Tree?

Tree Growth Rate Chart

Most trees grow an average of one inch in diameter each year. Some trees, like the ones below, grow more slowly. For example, mature American Elms take about four years to grow one inch in diameter. To estimate the age of a tree, find the tree in the list below and use the number shown in step 3 at right. If you don't see your tree below, use a growth rate factor of one.

American Elm 4
Ash 4
Aspen 2
Basswood 3
Black Cherry 5
Black Walnut 4.5
Cottonwood 2
Dogwood 7
Ironwood 7
Pin Oak 3
Red Oak 4
Redbud 7
Red Maple 4.5
River Birch 3.5
Shagbark Hickory 7.5
Silver Maple 3
Sugar Maple 5
White Birch 5
White Oak 5

Life-saving Trees

If you were lost in the woods, what would you do? How will you be found? Learn about the Hug-a-Tree program that suggests you hug a tree and stay with that tree until you are found. Kids, teachers, and rescuers alike are all learning how the "Hug a Tree" program works. Ask your teacher about this program or search the Internet for "Hug-a-tree."

Did you know that trees are the largest plants on earth? Some trees can grow to be thousands of years old and hundreds of feet high. You don't have to chop down a tree and count the rings to estimate its age. Try this little exercise on the biggest tree you see. You'll need a calculator and measuring tape. I hope you discover a really old tree.

1. From the base of the tree, measure $4\frac{1}{2}$ feet up the trunk. At the $4\frac{1}{2}$ foot mark, measure the distance around the trunk (the circumference). Write the circumference below (in inches):
   Circumference =

2. Use this formula to determine the diameter, (distance through the trunk) also called the Diameter at Breast Height, or DBH. Then write the DBH below (in inches):
   Circumference divided by 3.14 = DBH
   DBH=

3. Get the growth rate of your tree from the list in the sidebar (left). Then multiply your tree's diameter by its growth rate. The result is the approximate age of your tree. Here's your last formula. When you calculate the answer, write it below.
   Diameter x growth rate = age
   Approximate Age =

I couldn't even get my arms around this California Redwood. Have you ever seen a trunk so big?

How Tall Is That Tree?

Now that you know the approximate age of your tree, would you like to know its approximate height? You don't have to climb to the top of the tree with your measuring tape for this. In fact, I hope you don't—you know what they say on TV, "Don't try this at home!" Let's do this the safe way. You need pencil (you can use a stick if you don't have a pencil), a partner to help you, and a long measuring tape.

1. Stand far away from the tree facing it. Hold your arm straight out and your pencil straight up and walk toward the tree until it looks like it is the same size as your pencil.

2. Keeping your arm straight out in front of you, turn your pencil to a horizontal position so that one end appears to be touching the base of the tree.

3. Have your partner stand alongside the tree far enough away from the tree so that they appear to be standing on the other end of the pencil.

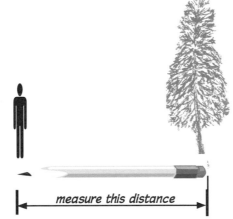

measure this distance

4. Mark where your partner is standing. Measure the distance from there to the base of the tree with your measuring tape. That measurement will be the tree's height.

Food and Shelter

Many animals depend on trees to give them shelter from wind and heavy rains. Can you think of any such animals? How about deer or moose?

Why Do Some Trees Die Young?

Different species of trees live for different lengths of time. Some trees live to be thousands of years old!

Of course, not all trees live to old age. Trees can be hit by lightning, or consumed by fire or insects. Trees are also cut down for lumber. Some trees die from disease and some diseases can kill hundreds, even thousands of trees.

Many of the killers of our trees (like fungi and insects) actually come from other countries and are carried into this country by accident. The American Elm (the state tree for Massachusetts and North Dakota) was nearly destroyed by a fungus that was spread by a beetle. The disease killed so many of our cherished American Elms that it's hard to find one today.

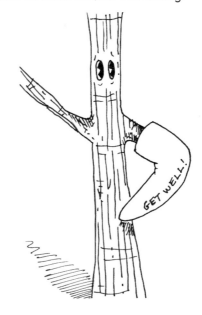

GET WELL!

Trees of Canada

Canada celebrates, too. Here's a list of the Provincial trees of Canada:

Alberta:
Lodgepole Pine

British Columbia:
Western Red Cedar

Manitoba:
White Spruce

New Brunswick:
Balsam Fir

Newfoundland:
Black Spruce

Northwest Territories:
Jack Pine

Nova Scotia:
Red Spruce

Nunavut:
(no official tree)

Ontario:
Eastern White Pine

Prince Edward Island:
Northern Red Oak

Quebec:
Yellow Birch

Saskatchewan:
Paper Birch

Yukon:
Quaking Aspen

L et's concentrate again on the trees you selected to identify. Look at the shape of your trees. Stand far enough away from the tree so you can see the whole tree. If you're in the woods, it might be difficult to tell the shape of a tree, and you'll have to depend on your observations of the trunk and leaves to ID it.

Trees come in lots of shapes and sizes: tall, skinny, short or round.

The shapes of conifers, or evergreens include (left to right) **pyramidal, conical,** *and* **columnar.**

Conifer shapes look like pyramids or cones or columns. Have you ever seen conifers covered with snow? Aren't they beautiful? Eighteen of our states have conifers as their state tree including Nevada (Bristlecone Pine), Arkansas (Pine), New Mexico (Pinyon), and Alabama and North Carolina (Longleaf Pine).

Broadleaf shapes include (clockwise from top left) **vase, spreading, rounded** *and* **broad.**

Broadleaf trees have some pretty distinct shapes, too. Look at the different shapes in these drawings. Broadleaf trees are popular shade trees in cities and towns. I used to live in a town where the streets are lined in dogwoods. Every year they have a dogwood festival and parade to celebrate the dogwoods in bloom. It was so beautiful!

When you decide on the shape of your tree turn to page 24 to begin your Tree Notes. Write in your trees' shapes, then return here.

Tree Bark

After you observe the shape of your trees, look at the bark. Look closely to observe the color and feel the texture. As you see here, not all bark is brown and smooth. Look at the curly bark on the Paper Birch. This tree supplies us with a very important building material—popsicle sticks!

Look at the bark of the American Sycamore. The outer bark can't grow as fast as the tree so it peels off and exposes the inner bark. On older sycamores, the trunk is almost all white.

The Hercules Club tree is nicknamed the "toothache tree" because it was used to numb the pain of a toothache. It's a strange looking bark, don't you think?

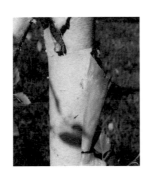

The Paper Birch is the state tree of New Hampshire.

The Hercules Club tree bumps grow to a certain size and then fall off.

The thorns (ouch!) on the Honey Locust tree make it easy to ID.

The Southern Catalpa bark has many ridges.

On old American Sycamores, the bark can be almost all white.

The Shagbark Hickory is easy to ID. No other bark looks quite like this.

Collecting Data

When Meri Schorr (age 11) took her first tree walk, she invited her Mom. It was spring and they collected flowers from a broadleaf tree. Meri wrote:

"The bark is brown, hard and flaky and the flowers have 4 light pink, stiff petals."

They also saw a conifer, which had a pyramidal shape, and they collected a small stem with leaves. Meri wrote this about the bark:

"Dark brown, rough and looks like peeling paint"

These are great descriptions. Thanks Meri!

The Shagbark Hickory is another tree easily identified by its bark. See how shaggy it is? The Shagbark Hickory is part of the Walnut Family of trees. Another member of that family is the Pecan tree, the state tree of Texas.

These examples of bark show you that bark comes in lots of textures and colors. Does your tree bark look like any of these? Sketch or describe the bark of your tree on the Tree Notes pages or take a picture of it if you can.

Popular Trees

Needle-leaf trees are very popular as Christmas trees. They are also popular as state trees. The state tree for Louisiana is the Baldcypress, which has a soft, flat, short needle-leaf. The state tree for Maine and Michigan is the Eastern White Pine, which has a long needle-leaf. The state tree for Idaho, the Western White Pine, also has a long needle-leaf and so does the Ponderosa Pine, state tree of Montana.

Some conifers grow one row of spreading branches a year. The distance from one row to the next is one year's growth. The Red Pine is such a tree and it's also the state tree of Minnesota.

What kind of leaves do your trees have? There are three major groups of leaves: the conifer, the broadleaf, and the yuccas and palms. Within these groups, leaves vary in shape, size, and color.

Conifers have two basic leaf shapes: *scale-leaf* and *needle-leaf*. A scale-leaf is flat and scaly. Cedars are scale-leaf trees.

The needle-leaf can be a long needle in a cluster or a short needle without clusters. If your tree has a needle-leaf in a cluster, be sure to count the number of needles in a cluster and write that down. This information will help you to identify your tree using a field guide. Examples of needle-leaf conifers are pine trees and spruce trees. The Blue Spruce is the state tree for both Colorado and Utah. Spruce is also the state tree for Alaska (Sitka Spruce) and South Dakota (White Spruce).

Leaves of the palms and yuccas can be shaped like fans, blades of grass or swords. Both palms and yuccas are evergreen.

Find your leaf shape on these pages; then draw your leaf on your Tree Notes page. Use the drawings here as a guide and don't forget to put the name of the leaf shape on your drawing. You can also gather some leaves in your collection bag and glue them onto your tree pages when you get home.

A scale-leaf has short, overlapping leaves arranged along twigs.

A needle-leaf can grow in clusters (left) or as single needles (right).

Palm and Yucca leaves are fanlike, and easy to recognize. The Cabbage Palmetto shown here is the state tree for two states: Florida and South Carolina.

...And Broadleaf Trees

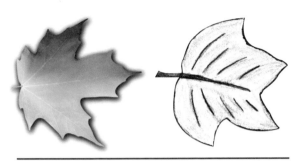

Broadleaf trees have two basic leaf types: *simple* and *compound*. A simple leaf is a single leaf on a stem—such as a maple or oak leaf. A simple leaf can be lobed, which means it has projections or indentations along its edges like a maple or poplar leaf. If a simple leaf has jagged edges or pointed stickers on its edges, it's a simple toothed leaf. A simple leaf with a single blade, smooth edges, and no lobes, is a simple untoothed leaf.

Simple lobed

Simple toothed

Simple untoothed

A compound leaf looks like many leaves together but it's really a leaf made up of smaller leaves (leaflets). If the leaflets are attached on the stem along the length of a single stalk, they are called *pinnately* compound. If the leaflets are attached at the same place on the stem, they are called *palmately* compound.

Pinnately compound

Palmately compound

Matt's Maples

Matt Kravitz (age 11) wrote this about his first tree walk:

"I did not have to go very far because there are a lot of beautiful old trees in and around my yard. The maple trees are the nicest feature of my yard. On a hot summer day they provide us with shade. I love to lie down in the hammock and look up. I see many shades of green and the sun filters through as the birds fly back and forth through the trees. In the fall they turn a beautiful shade of orange yellow. We have so much fun making huge leaf piles and kicking the piles! In the winter I hang a bird feeder. I love to watch the red cardinals eat the seeds."

Leaf Colors

Yellow Poplar

Sugar Maple

Sweetgum

White Oak

Black Maple

American Holly

Red Maple

Flowering Dogwood

Black Tupelo

What color are the leaves on your selected trees? Leaves come in many different shades of green, and in the fall the leaves of many broadleaf trees change color. A field guide to trees for the eastern half of the U.S. often contains a section to help you ID a tree by the color of its fall leaves.

Have you ever wondered why leaves change color in the fall and why some turn red, while others turn yellow or orange or gold? Well, leaves contain **pigments**, the natural substances that create their color.

Three pigments can be found in leaves. The first is chlorophyll (KLOR-a-fill), which turns the leaves green. The second is carotene (CARE-eh-teen), which turns leaves yellow, orange, or brown. The third pigment is anthocyanin (an-tho-CY-a-nin), which turns the leaves red. Anthocyanins are not in the leaves year-round but are produced by the changing weather and sunlight in the fall. In the summer when the weather is warm and we have long, sunny days, chlorophyll is at work in the leaves, making them green and helping the trees to produce food. As autumn approaches and the days become shorter with less sunlight, trees can't produce as much chlorophyll. When this happens the carotene and anthocyanins take over and change the colors of the leaves.

The leaves shown here are some of the most colorful in the fall. The Red Maple is changing from green to red—isn't it cool? The Red Maple is the state tree for Rhode Island.

Some broadleaf trees are evergreen; their leaves don't change color and they don't shed in the fall. One such evergreen is the American Holly, which is the state tree of Delaware.

Leaf Factoids and Oddities

The leaf shape and color are important keys to identifying a tree, but don't forget to observe the size of the leaf. Is the leaf as big as the palm of your hand? Is it longer than your longest finger? Write this information on your Tree Notes pages.

How are the leaves arranged on their branch? Most trees grow their leaves in an alternating pattern, which means one leaf grows above (or below) the other on the branch. Other trees grow their leaves in an opposite pattern where two leaves grow out from the same position on the branch directly across from each other.

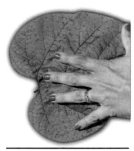

This Southern Catalpa leaf is bigger than my hand!

What is the texture of your leaf? Is it glossy or shiny, leathery, or fuzzy? Write the description on your Tree Notes pages.

There are some pretty unusual trees and leaves. The Ginkgo is an unusual tree. It's the only living species of its ancient family. There are male and female Ginkgo trees. The male tree has cones and the female tree has stinky seeds! A native of China, the Ginkgo tree is related to conifers.

The Ginkgo leaves look like little fans.

Some trees can look very different in different seasons. The dogwood tree has flowers in the spring, green leaves and berries in the summer. The berries last into the fall and are an important food source for birds. The leaves turn red in the fall. Visit your trees again in a different season so you can see how they change.

If it seems too difficult to ID a tree, don't give up. Take good notes and ask your teacher or parent for help.

Here's a dogwood tree in three seasons: spring, summer and fall. The white petals of the flower are actually leaf-like plant parts called bracts. Bracts protect the flower, which, in this case, is the little green center. The dogwood is the state tree of Missouri and Virginia.

Chlorophyll Test

Here's a fun test you can perform that will show you the importance of chlorophyll. When the broadleaf trees have leaves of green, take a small strip of black or dark paper and tape it to the leaf. Don't pick the leaf from the tree. In a few days, take off the paper. Is your leaf still green under the paper?

Green Bananas

You probably know that bananas grow on trees, but did you know bananas contain chlorophyll? As bananas ripen the chlorophyll disappears. The banana turns from green to yellow just like some leaves in the autumn.

Silly Tree Riddles:

I love silly riddles and here are some very silly ones: The answers are on the sidebar of the facing page.

1. Which trees can grow higher than a house?

2. What is part pig and part tree?

3. Why is a tree surgeon like an actor?

4. What did the tree say to the lumberjack?

5. The more of these you take, the more you leave behind— what are they?

Flowers, seeds, and fruits are the parts of the tree that help it reproduce itself. The flowers become the fruit and the fruit contains the seed.

Broadleaf trees can be as beautiful in the spring as they are in the fall, thanks to their spring flowers. One of the most beautiful sights in spring is the mass of pink flowers on the Eastern Redbud (state tree of Oklahoma). The Redbud is related to the Cottonwood, the state tree of Kansas, and the Eastern Cottonwood, state tree of Nebraska and Wyoming.

Fruits can be small berries or large, fleshy fruits. Some berry-like fruits are the Mountain Winterberry and the Southern Magnolia (the state tree of Mississippi). Fleshy fruits include pears, peaches, and apples.

Conifers don't bear fruit; they bear cones. They have male and female cones! The female cones are the large, woody cones and they contain the seed. The male cones are small and not woody. Both cones shown here are female. The Eastern White Pine cone is a large female cone, and the Eastern Hemlock (state tree of Pennsylvania) is a small female cone. The Eastern Hemlock is a relative of the Western Hemlock, which is the state tree of Washington.

To learn how you can see the seeds of a conifer, read the sidebar on the following page.

Flowers

American Basswood   Eastern Redbud

Berry-like Fruit

Mountain Winterberry   Southern Magnolia

Fleshy Fruit

Pear Tree   Crabapple Tree

Cones

Eastern White Pine   Eastern Hemlock

Seeds and Nuts

The seed-bearing fruit of a broadleaf can be a key, ball, pod, nut, or acorn, just to name a few.

A key is a single seed contained in a dry, flat covering. Maple and ash trees both have keys. (Hey, that rhymes!)

The fruit of a Sweetgum tree is a ball containing many individual fruits, each ending in long, prickly points (ouch).

The fruit of the American Sycamore is a bristly ball.

Pods are dry fruits usually shaped like a long cylinder containing several seeds. When the pod ripens the seams split open and the seeds fall out. Examples of trees with pods are the Honey Locust and the Northern Catalpa.

A nut is a seed contained inside a hard shell. Depending on the species of tree, a shell might contain more than one nut. Examples of trees with nuts are the KuKui tree, state tree of Hawaii, and the Ohio Buckeye, state tree of—you guessed it—Ohio!

An acorn is a nut with a point on one end and a scaly cap on the other. Shown here are acorns of the Pin Oak and the Northern Red Oak, the state tree of New Jersey.

Keys

Maple Keys   White Ash

Balls

Sweetgum   American Sycamore

Pods

Honey Locust   Northern Catalpa

Nuts

Kukui   Ohio Buckeye

Acorns

Pin Oak   Northern Red Oak

Where's the Seed?

Would you like to see the seeds of a conifer? Choose a tree where some cones have opened and others are still closed. Pick a closed cone— one that looks like it might be about to open— and bring it home. Put your cone in a paper bag. (Don't use plastic; it will retain moisture.) After a few days, the cone should open and the seeds will fall to the bottom of the bag.

Answers:

1. All trees—a house can't grow!

2. A Porky pine.

3. Because he's always taking boughs.

4. Leaf me alone

5. Footsteps

New Words?

Nutrients (NEW-tree-ents)

Minerals that help make the tree strong and healthy.

Cambium (CAM-bee-um)

A thin layer of living tissue between the bark and the wood of a tree.

In Other Words?

Another name for inner bark is phloem (FLO-em) and another word for sapwood is xylem (ZY-lem).

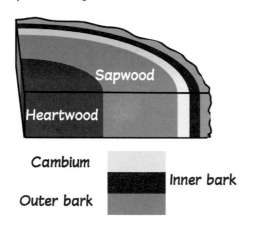

Tall Trees

Have you ever noticed that in the woods, some trees have very, very tall trunks and very skinny crowns? That's because trees crowd each other in the woods and they can't spread out to catch sunlight. To reach the sunlight, they must grow straight up.

Sunny Days

Here's what Trev Walklett (age 11) wrote about his tree walk:

"I love sitting under my weeping willow in the summer just reading in the shade."

Now that you've observed the many different parts of a tree, let's put them all together to see how a tree works.

Starting at the bottom, the roots soak up water and *nutrients*, which flow through the *sapwood* all the way up to the leaves.

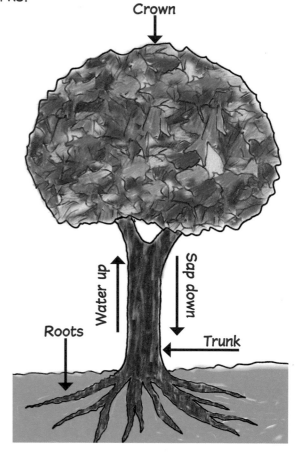

The leaves and the branches make up the crown. The branches hold the leaves up to help them get as much sunlight as possible so they can produce the tree's food, called sap. Sap flows from the leaves through the inner bark all the way down to the roots.

Look at the drawing in the sidebar to the left. You can see that between the sapwood and the inner bark is the **cambium**, which creates new sapwood and inner bark. As the cambium adds new sapwood, tree rings are formed (one per year). As the cambium adds new inner bark, older inner bark becomes outer bark.

As the sapwood ages, water stops flowing through it and it becomes *heartwood*. Heartwood is located in the center of the trunk and is usually darker colored than the younger sapwood.

...Together

You've finished your tree walk—did you see lots of trees today? How many trees did you know and list on page six? If you knew four different kinds of trees before you started reading this book, that's pretty good! Have you seen other trees today that you recognize? Did you write them down?

Trees can change a lot from season to season. Visit your trees again in a different season so you can make new drawings and record additional information about the trees.

Perhaps you've been able to ID some trees today based on the photos in this book. If there are trees you did not recognize, write about them on page 25 in your Tree Notes.

When you get home, use a field guide and ask an older family member for some help to ID the trees. If you don't have a field guide, you can check one out at your local library.

Look at this grove of Tamarack trees—it's autumn and the trees have dropped their leaves. The Tamarack is a conifer but it is deciduous. Its needles change colors and drop in the fall.

A Cord of Wood

Firewood is usually measured by the cord. A cord of wood is four feet high, four feet wide and eight feet long. One cord of wood can make:

7,500,000 toothpicks, or

250 copies of the NY Times Sunday paper or

12 dining room tables.

Tree Poetry

**"I think that I shall never see
A poem as lovely as a tree."**

These are the last two lines of Joyce Kilmer's famous poem called "trees." Have you ever heard this poem? It's very beautiful. I think that I feel just like Joyce Kilmer (who, by the way, was a man) when it comes to trees. To learn more about this poet and this poem, ask your teacher, librarian, or parents to help you, or search for "Joyce Kilmer" on the web.

Can Trees Grow in the Desert?

You bet they can! Nature designed trees for the desert that are tolerant of the heat and that don't need as much water as other species. In the desert you can find the Whitethorn Acacia, the Ironwood tree and the Mesquite.

Completing Your Tree Notes

The illustration on this page shows you how you can use your Tree Notes pages. You can also paste photos or leaves on the page. In the top example, the bark, cone, leaf and full tree are drawn along with notes about each.

The example of tree notes is shown here on the right. This example of a Yellow Poplar shows the flower, seeds, and the colors of leaves in summer and fall. You won't see all these parts of a tree in one season. Visit your tree at different times of the year to observe it. The Yellow Poplar is the state tree of three states: Kentucky, Indiana, and Tennessee.

Here's an example of how you might fill in your Tree Notes page.

Date: June 15

Tree location: Back Yard

Tree shape: An oval-round shape.
This is a very tall tree with a very straight trunk.

Circle one: (Broadleaf) or conifer

Bark color and texture: Dark gray with deep furrows.

Leaf Type: broadleaf, very wide with simple lobes.

Leaf color: Dark green on top, pale underneath,

Flower or seed description: There are flowers which look sort of like tulips. There is no fruit on the tree at this time of year but I drew it from memory. The cone shaped fruit appears in the fall and sometimes stays on the tree most of the winter.

Tree Name: Yellow Poplar

Yellow poplar
"Tuliptree"

Leaves: 3-6 in long, 4 to 6 lobes, shiny green on top, pale green below, yellow in autumn
Bark: Dark grey
Flowers: long and wide, cup shaped.
Cone-like fruit

Spring + Summer

Flower

seeds

Fall

Tree Notes

Date:

Tree location:

Tree shape:

Circle one: Broadleaf or conifer

Bark color and texture:

Leaf Type:

Leaf color:

Flower or seed description:

Tree Name:

As Good as a Photo

Our friend Lauren Frail (age 11) wrote this about a tree she observed on her tree walk:

"The tree doesn't have many leaves but the leaves are a jungle green. The bark is grayish brown in color. The flowers are a clean white and they're soft like silk. In the centers of the flowers are green balls."

Lauren's description of the tree's flowers was so good, I knew which tree she was describing. Lauren found her tree in a field guide and identified it as a flowering dogwood. She was right!

Meet Allison Sauls

Here's what Allison Sauls wrote to us about her experience in the National Arbor Day Poster Contest:

"The inspiration to enter the contest came from my art teacher, Mrs. Judy Johnson. When I won, I was invited to Washington, D.C. to attend the unveiling ceremony where the National Tree for the United States was announced—that was a really big honor! At the unveiling ceremony, I met a lot of dignitaries and politicians and I helped plant a Red Oak on the grounds of the capitol. I think it is special that when I am old and have grandchildren I can travel to Washington, D.C. and look at the tree I helped plant with all those officials. I am really pleased to have been a little part of history. I got to meet a lot of cool people who care for trees and our environment. My favorite tree is the Ginkgo Biloba tree. It has been around since the dinosaur days and I think that's really cool! It also has magnificent leaves, and I voted for it for the National Tree. But the oak tree won, which is OK because I learned that there are oak trees in 49 of the 50 states and I know that the Ginkgo Biloba only grows in some states.".

Treasures in the Tree

Have you seen any nests today? Rachel Loia (age 11) wrote about a nest.

"On my walk, I wrote about one tree while I was sitting in it! I discovered a bird's nest with two robin's eggs in it. That was a really cool thing to find."

People around the world celebrate the beauty and value of trees in many ways: through songs and poems, paintings and books. In the U.S. we have a national tree-planting holiday called Arbor Day—the idea of J. Sterling Morton of Nebraska, a long, long time ago. On the first Arbor Day in 1872, more than one million trees were planted in Nebraska alone!

Today, the National Arbor Day Foundation carries on the work of Mr. Morton. It is the largest tree-planting environmental organization in the world. The foundation provides more than 8 million trees for planting throughout America each year. National Arbor Day is celebrated every year on the last Friday in April. You can learn more at **www.arborday.org.**

Every year, the National Arbor Day Foundation has a poster contest for fifth graders from all over the U.S. Here is a winning National Arbor Day Foundation poster, created by Allison Sauls (age 11). Over 59,000 fifth grade classrooms participate in the contest. Read more about Allison in the sidebar of this page.

Questions?

When I visit schools all over the U.S., kids always have lots of questions about trees. Here are three of the most-asked and my answers:

- **Why do leaves fall in the autumn?**
  The leaves of deciduous trees are delicate and begin falling when temperatures drop below freezing (below 32 degrees Fahrenheit or zero degrees Celsius). Leaves contain water and sap. As the sunlight decreases in the fall, the leaves produce less sap. A layer forms between the base of the leaf and the branch to which it is attached. This is called the separation layer. As this layer grows, it seals the leaf from the branch and the leaf eventually falls to the ground. This is nature's way of protecting the tree during the cold winter, so it doesn't lose water.

- **What is the oldest tree in the United States?**
  According to the American Forests Organization, the oldest tree on record is a Western Juniper located in Stanislaus National Forest, California. The tree is about 4,000 years old. California has many of our champion trees, but Florida has the most! Learn more about champion trees and interesting tree facts at: **www.americanforests.org.**

- **Does maple syrup really come from maple trees?**
  Yes, it does! Maple syrup really does come from maple trees. You can learn more from The Massachusetts Maple Producers Association, **www.massmaple.org.**

Books for You:

Here are some great books whose stories are about appreciating and enjoying trees. I hope you get to read one soon.

The Man Who Planted Trees

By Jean Giono. Chelsea Green Publishing Company.

This is a story about a man who planted 100 acorns every day of his adult life and transformed a sorrowful place into one full of life and joy. This book can show you how one person can make a big difference in the lives of others!

The Giving Tree

By Shel Silverstein. HarperCollins Juvenile Books.

This story is about the relationship of a man and a tree throughout the man's life. It's a wonderful story!

The Lorax

By Dr. Seuss. Random House.

I bet you read Dr. Seuss books when you were little. Did you ever read this one? This is about saving trees. If you feel like you're too old to enjoy Dr. Seuss, maybe you could read this book to someone younger. After all, Dr. Seuss books are best when read aloud, don't you think?

The Swiss Family Robinson

By Johann David Wyss. Yearling Books.

An exciting story about a shipwrecked family and their adventures. They must learn to survive off the land and live with nature. Guess where they build their house? In a tree!

Tree Careers

How many careers are there that focus on trees? Quite a few! Would you like to do this kind of work someday?

Dendrologist (den-DRAH-low-jist):

A person who specializes in identifying trees and determining the age of trees.

Arborist (AR-bor-ist):

A tree specialist who is an expert in the growth and care of trees.

Forester (FOUR-is-ter):

A person who takes care of our forests and who works to keep them healthy. This job can include planting trees, managing forest fires, and protecting trees from disease.

Firefighter:

A person who helps to control wildfires. Firefighters who parachute into a remote area to help control wildfires are called smokejumpers

Landscaper:

A person who plants trees and other plants to make the areas around homes and buildings beautiful.

Silviculturist

(SIL-va-cul-cher-ist):

A person who studies the connection and impact of a forest to its environment and who manages the care and reproduction of trees.

Logger:

A person who cuts down trees and transports them to sawmills where they are cut into wood materials.

Other than the organizations mentioned in this book, do you know who else works to protect trees? When your tree walk is over, search the Internet or go to your local library to learn about other organizations that work to protect and educate people about trees. Perhaps you and your family will want to join one of those important organizations, such as the National Audubon Society or the Nature Conservancy.

Here are some other fun activities to do when your walk is over:

✓ **Learn about tree rings.** Find out what they are and what they tell us about trees and climate.

✓ **Find the state trees.** Find and list all of the state trees mentioned in this book. All fifty are here. Can you tell which tree is the most popular state tree and how many states it represents?

✓ **Start a leaf collection.** Collect leaves and put them in an album, labeling them with their tree species. Or place leaves between pieces of tissue paper (not the Kleenex type) and rub the paper with the side of your pencil to create a leaf drawing. Or you can make leaf prints by applying washable paint to the veined side of a leaf and pressing the leaf onto a piece of paper.

✓ **Become a friend of trees.** Take a friend on a tree walk. Share the beauty and importance of trees with them; tell them what you've learned about trees. Help them to become a friend of trees, too.

✓ **Group your trees.** Remember the list of tree names you created on page six? Return to that page and write down which of your trees are broadleaf trees and which are conifers.

...To Do

✓ **Visit an arboretum** (are-bore-EAT-um)—a place where many kinds of trees and bushes are grown for scientific study or for people to see and enjoy. Ask your parents if there is an arboretum near you and if they will take you there. Visiting an arboretum is a great way to see many trees and to help you identify trees. It's also a good place to take a tree walk.

✓ **Build a tree house.** If you have a big old tree in your yard, talk with your parents about building a tree house. If building a tree house isn't an option, how about building a tree house for the birds? Put up a nesting box, a bird feeder, or a squirrel feeder. Don't put both bird and squirrel feeders on the same tree—the squirrels will eat the birdseed.

Christian Conard (age 10) drew this tree house complete with a bird house! It looks like a great place to hang out, doesn't it? I love his attention to detail—he even included the curtains.

If you like these ideas or you have some of your own, write them on your Ideas and Questions page. When you return home, you can find the answers to your questions from your parents, teachers, the library, or the Internet.

Websites to Visit

Visit these Websites for more information on trees and tree observation.

treelink.org/whattree

Find your tree by identifying its leaves.

forestry.about.com

Features news about forests and trees, forest firefighting, and tree diseases. You learn about individual tree species here and read about tree planting or Smokey the Bear.

enature.com

The tree flashcards at eNature are the coolest. You can find a tree by first selecting the type of leaf or by typing in its name.

Keyword Searches

To find more Websites about trees, search using the following keywords:

trees

forestry

arboretum

or try names of specific trees, such as "oak" or "maple"

What to Write

List any questions you have about your tree walk today. When you return home, find the answers to your questions by asking your teacher or parents, or by searching the library or Internet.

List ideas that came to you today. If you want to visit a tree again in another season, write that down. If you think you'll need directions to find the tree again, write the directions on this page.

State Trees

Find the state trees in this book and fill in each state tree after the abbreviated state name on the right. If you don't know the state abbreviations,

AL
AK
AR
AZ
CA
CO
CT
DE
FL
GA
HI
ID
IL
IN
IO
KS
KY
LA
MA
MD
ME
MI
MN
MS
MO
MT
NB
NH
NJ
NM
NV
NY
ND
NC
OH
OK
OR
PA
RI
SC
SD
TN
TX
UT
VT
VA
WA
WV
WI
WY